MY
BOOK
JOURNAL

A 100-Book Reading
Diary for Bibliophiles

STERLING
New York

STERLING
New York

An Imprint of Sterling Publishing, Co., Inc.
1166 Avenue of the Americas
New York, NY 10016

ISBN: 978-1-4549-3633-6

Distributed in Canada by Sterling Publishing Co., Inc.
c/o Canadian Manda Group, 664 Annette Street
Toronto, Ontario M6S 2C8, Canada
Distributed in the United Kingdom by GMC Distribution Services
Castle Place, 166 High Street, Lewes, East Sussex BN7 1XU, England
Distributed in Australia by NewSouth Books
University of New South Wales, Sydney, NSW 2052, Australia

For information about custom editions, special sales,
and premium and corporate purchases, please contact Sterling Special Sales
at 800-805-5489 or specialsales@sterlingpublishing.com.

Manufactured in China

2 4 6 8 10 9 7 5 3 1

sterlingpublishing.com

Cover and interior design by Scott Russo
Text written and compiled by Barbara M. Berger

Picture credits—see page 192

CONTENTS

INTRODUCTION

"I declare after all
there is no enjoyment like reading!
How much sooner one tires
of any thing than of a book!"

—Jane Austen, *Pride and Prejudice*

HOW TO USE *MY BOOK JOURNAL*

This keepsake journal is the perfect place to chronicle your literary journey. Organized into six parts, you can keep track of what books you've read, what you think about them, and what books you want to read in the future.

Start off with the first section, **Books Read—My Table of Contents**. Once you finish a book, enter its title in the numbered list, and then go to the corresponding numbered page in **My Reading Log**. For example, if the first book you want to enter is *Don Quixote*, you would enter "*Don Quixote*" on the first line of the numbered list on page 6 after the numeral "1." Then you would go to page 12 in My Reading Log, and fill out the page for Title 1 with your review of *Don Quixote* and details about the book.

You can get some fun ideas about what books to read next in the section called **Book Challenges**. You'll find 24 challenges there that could inspire you to discover some new genres or subjects you've always wanted to try. Check them off in the little boxes as you read them, and fill in your notes on the experience.

My Book Lists is the next section, one that you can complete at your leisure. Create a mini time capsule of your own personal views by filling out 24 lists of your top 10s in a wide range of categories, from your 10 favorite book characters to your 10 favorite book-based movies or TV shows to the 10 scariest books you've read.

Best Book Lists—Prizewinners and Classics contains lists of Modern Library's 100 best fiction and 100 best nonfiction books, as well as a list of the 92 books that have won the Pulitzer Prize for fiction, and the 51 books that have won the Man Booker Prize for fiction (through 2018). There are boxes next to each title that you can check off once you read them (or if you've read them in the past).

The Book Club section contains space to enter up to 20 titles to get the reading list for your club started out, along with questions to help facilitate discussion and space for notes.

Finally, the last part, **Wish List of Books to Read**, provides space for you to list the books you want to read in the future.

Happy reading!

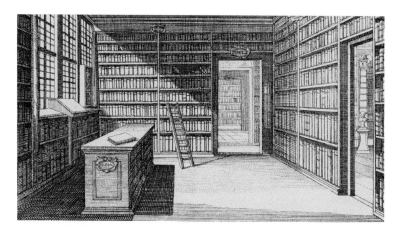

BOOKS READ:
MY TABLE OF CONTENTS

BOOK TITLES

1. A Song of Ice + Fire : A Game of Thrones
2. A Song of Ice + Fire : A Clash of Kings
3.
4.
5.
6.
7.
8.
9.
10.
11.
12.
13.
14.
15.
16.
17.
18.
19.

BOOK TITLES

20. _____
21. _____
22. _____
23. _____
24. _____
25. _____
26. _____
27. _____
28. _____
29. _____
30. _____
31. _____
32. _____
33. _____
34. _____
35. _____
36. _____
37. _____
38. _____
39. _____
40. _____
41. _____

BOOK TITLES

42. _____
43. _____
44. _____
45. _____
46. _____
47. _____
48. _____
49. _____
50. _____
51. _____
52. _____
53. _____
54. _____
55. _____
56. _____
57. _____
58. _____
59. _____
60. _____
61. _____
62. _____
63. _____

BOOK TITLES

64. _____

65. _____

66. _____

67. _____

68. _____

69. _____

70. _____

71. _____

72. _____

73. _____

74. _____

75. _____

76. _____

77. _____

78. _____

79. _____

80. _____

81. _____

82. _____

83. _____

84. _____

85. _____

BOOK TITLES

86. _____

87. _____

88. _____

89. _____

90. _____

91. _____

92. _____

93. _____

94. _____

95. _____

96. _____

97. _____

98. _____

99. _____

100. _____

MY
READING LOG

"Dreams, books, are each a world;
And books, we know,
Are a substantial world,
both pure and good."

—William Wordsworth

1. TITLE

Start date: _8/7/2020_ Finish date: _____

Author(s): _George R. R. Martin_

Publisher: _Bantam Books_ Year published: _1996_

Fiction/Genre: _Fiction?_ or Nonfiction/Category: _____

Where I bought, borrowed, or found the book: _Christmas 2019_

Main character(s) or subject: _a lot_

My review and thoughts: _____

_____

_____

_____

_____

_____

_____

_____

_____

_____

_____

_____

_____

OVERALL RATING: Quality of writing ☆☆☆☆☆
Strength of characters ☆☆☆☆☆ Plot ☆☆☆☆☆

2. TITLE

Start date: _____ Finish date: _____

Author(s): _____

Publisher: _____ Year published: _____

Fiction/Genre: _____ or Nonfiction/Category: _____

Where I bought, borrowed, or found the book: _____

Main character(s) or subject: _____

My review and thoughts: _____

_____

_____

_____

_____

_____

_____

_____

_____

_____

_____

_____

_____

OVERALL RATING: Quality of writing ☆☆☆☆☆
Strength of characters ☆☆☆☆☆ Plot ☆☆☆☆☆

3. TITLE

Start date: _____ Finish date: _____

Author(s): _____

Publisher: _____ Year published: _____

Fiction/Genre: _____ or Nonfiction/Category: _____

Where I bought, borrowed, or found the book: _____

Main character(s) or subject: _____

My review and thoughts: _____

_____

_____

_____

_____

_____

_____

_____

_____

_____

_____

_____

_____

OVERALL RATING: Quality of writing ☆☆☆☆☆
Strength of characters ☆☆☆☆☆ Plot ☆☆☆☆☆

4. TITLE

Start date: _____ Finish date: _____

Author(s): _____

Publisher: _____ Year published: _____

Fiction/Genre: _____ or Nonfiction/Category: _____

Where I bought, borrowed, or found the book: _____

Main character(s) or subject: _____

My review and thoughts: _____

_____

_____

_____

_____

_____

_____

_____

_____

_____

_____

_____

OVERALL RATING: Quality of writing ☆☆☆☆☆
Strength of characters ☆☆☆☆☆ Plot ☆☆☆☆☆

5. TITLE

Start date: _____ Finish date: _____

Author(s): _____

Publisher: _____ Year published: _____

Fiction/Genre: _____ or Nonfiction/Category: _____

Where I bought, borrowed, or found the book: _____

Main character(s) or subject: _____

My review and thoughts: _____

_____

_____

_____

_____

_____

_____

_____

_____

_____

_____

_____

OVERALL RATING: Quality of writing ☆☆☆☆☆
Strength of characters ☆☆☆☆☆ Plot ☆☆☆☆☆

6. TITLE

Start date: _____ Finish date: _____

Author(s): _____

Publisher: _____ Year published: _____

Fiction/Genre: _____ or Nonfiction/Category: _____

Where I bought, borrowed, or found the book: _____

Main character(s) or subject: _____

My review and thoughts: _____

_____

_____

_____

_____

_____

_____

_____

_____

_____

_____

_____

OVERALL RATING: Quality of writing ☆☆☆☆☆
Strength of characters ☆☆☆☆☆ Plot ☆☆☆☆☆

7. TITLE

Start date: _____ Finish date: _____

Author(s): _____

Publisher: _____ Year published: _____

Fiction/Genre: _____ or Nonfiction/Category: _____

Where I bought, borrowed, or found the book: _____

Main character(s) or subject: _____

My review and thoughts: _____

_____

_____

_____

_____

_____

_____

_____

_____

_____

_____

_____

OVERALL RATING: Quality of writing ☆☆☆☆☆
Strength of characters ☆☆☆☆☆ Plot ☆☆☆☆☆

8. TITLE

Start date: _____ Finish date: _____

Author(s): _____

Publisher: _____ Year published: _____

Fiction/Genre: _____ or Nonfiction/Category: _____

Where I bought, borrowed, or found the book: _____

Main character(s) or subject: _____

My review and thoughts: _____

_____

_____

_____

_____

_____

_____

_____

_____

_____

_____

_____

OVERALL RATING: Quality of writing ☆☆☆☆☆
Strength of characters ☆☆☆☆☆ Plot ☆☆☆☆☆

9. TITLE

Start date: _____ Finish date: _____

Author(s): _____

Publisher: _____ Year published: _____

Fiction/Genre: _____ or Nonfiction/Category: _____

Where I bought, borrowed, or found the book: _____

Main character(s) or subject: _____

My review and thoughts: _____

_____

_____

_____

_____

_____

_____

_____

_____

_____

_____

_____

_____

OVERALL RATING: Quality of writing ☆☆☆☆☆
Strength of characters ☆☆☆☆☆ Plot ☆☆☆☆☆

10. TITLE

Start date: _____ Finish date: _____

Author(s): _____

Publisher: _____ Year published: _____

Fiction/Genre: _____ or Nonfiction/Category: _____

Where I bought, borrowed, or found the book: _____

Main character(s) or subject: _____

My review and thoughts: _____

_____

_____

_____

_____

_____

_____

_____

_____

_____

_____

_____

OVERALL RATING: Quality of writing ☆☆☆☆☆
Strength of characters ☆☆☆☆☆ Plot ☆☆☆☆☆

11. TITLE

Start date: _____ Finish date: _____

Author(s): _____

Publisher: _____ Year published: _____

Fiction/Genre: _____ or Nonfiction/Category: _____

Where I bought, borrowed, or found the book: _____

Main character(s) or subject: _____

My review and thoughts: _____

_____

_____

_____

_____

_____

_____

_____

_____

_____

_____

_____

_____

OVERALL RATING: Quality of writing ☆☆☆☆☆
Strength of characters ☆☆☆☆☆ Plot ☆☆☆☆☆

12. TITLE

Start date: _____ Finish date: _____

Author(s): _____

Publisher: _____ Year published: _____

Fiction/Genre: _____ or Nonfiction/Category: _____

Where I bought, borrowed, or found the book: _____

Main character(s) or subject: _____

My review and thoughts: _____

_____

_____

_____

_____

_____

_____

_____

_____

_____

_____

_____

_____

OVERALL RATING: Quality of writing ☆☆☆☆☆
Strength of characters ☆☆☆☆☆ Plot ☆☆☆☆☆

13. TITLE

Start date: _____ Finish date: _____

Author(s): _____

Publisher: _____ Year published: _____

Fiction/Genre: _____ or Nonfiction/Category: _____

Where I bought, borrowed, or found the book: _____

Main character(s) or subject: _____

My review and thoughts: _____

_____

_____

_____

_____

_____

_____

_____

_____

_____

_____

_____

_____

OVERALL RATING: Quality of writing ☆☆☆☆☆
Strength of characters ☆☆☆☆☆ Plot ☆☆☆☆☆

14. TITLE

Start date: _____ Finish date: _____

Author(s): _____

Publisher: _____ Year published: _____

Fiction/Genre: _____ or Nonfiction/Category: _____

Where I bought, borrowed, or found the book: _____

Main character(s) or subject: _____

My review and thoughts: _____

_____

_____

_____

_____

_____

_____

_____

_____

_____

_____

_____

_____

_____

OVERALL RATING: Quality of writing ☆☆☆☆☆
Strength of characters ☆☆☆☆☆ Plot ☆☆☆☆☆

15. TITLE

Start date: _____ Finish date: _____

Author(s): _____

Publisher: _____ Year published: _____

Fiction/Genre: _____ or Nonfiction/Category: _____

Where I bought, borrowed, or found the book: _____

Main character(s) or subject: _____

My review and thoughts: _____

_____

_____

_____

_____

_____

_____

_____

_____

_____

_____

_____

OVERALL RATING: Quality of writing ☆☆☆☆☆
Strength of characters ☆☆☆☆☆ Plot ☆☆☆☆☆

16. TITLE

Start date: _____ Finish date: _____

Author(s): _____

Publisher: _____ Year published: _____

Fiction/Genre: _____ or Nonfiction/Category: _____

Where I bought, borrowed, or found the book: _____

Main character(s) or subject: _____

My review and thoughts: _____

_____

_____

_____

_____

_____

_____

_____

_____

_____

_____

_____

_____

OVERALL RATING: Quality of writing ☆☆☆☆☆
Strength of characters ☆☆☆☆☆ Plot ☆☆☆☆☆

17. TITLE

Start date: _____ Finish date: _____

Author(s): _____

Publisher: _____ Year published: _____

Fiction/Genre: _____ or Nonfiction/Category: _____

Where I bought, borrowed, or found the book: _____

Main character(s) or subject: _____

My review and thoughts: _____

_____

_____

_____

_____

_____

_____

_____

_____

_____

_____

_____

OVERALL RATING: Quality of writing ☆☆☆☆☆
Strength of characters ☆☆☆☆☆ Plot ☆☆☆☆☆

18. TITLE

Start date: _____ Finish date: _____

Author(s): _____

Publisher: _____ Year published: _____

Fiction/Genre: _____ or Nonfiction/Category: _____

Where I bought, borrowed, or found the book: _____

Main character(s) or subject: _____

My review and thoughts: _____

_____

_____

_____

_____

_____

_____

_____

_____

_____

_____

_____

OVERALL RATING: Quality of writing ☆☆☆☆☆
Strength of characters ☆☆☆☆☆ Plot ☆☆☆☆☆

19. TITLE

Start date: _____ Finish date: _____

Author(s): _____

Publisher: _____ Year published: _____

Fiction/Genre: _____ or Nonfiction/Category: _____

Where I bought, borrowed, or found the book: _____

Main character(s) or subject: _____

My review and thoughts: _____

_____

_____

_____

_____

_____

_____

_____

_____

_____

_____

_____

OVERALL RATING: Quality of writing ☆☆☆☆☆
Strength of characters ☆☆☆☆☆ Plot ☆☆☆☆☆

20. TITLE

Start date: _____ Finish date: _____

Author(s): _____

Publisher: _____ Year published: _____

Fiction/Genre: _____ or Nonfiction/Category: _____

Where I bought, borrowed, or found the book: _____

Main character(s) or subject: _____

My review and thoughts: _____

_____

_____

_____

_____

_____

_____

_____

_____

_____

_____

_____

OVERALL RATING: Quality of writing ☆☆☆☆☆
Strength of characters ☆☆☆☆☆ Plot ☆☆☆☆☆

21. TITLE

Start date: _____ Finish date: _____

Author(s): _____

Publisher: _____ Year published: _____

Fiction/Genre: _____ or Nonfiction/Category: _____

Where I bought, borrowed, or found the book: _____

Main character(s) or subject: _____

My review and thoughts: _____

_____

_____

_____

_____

_____

_____

_____

_____

_____

_____

_____

_____

OVERALL RATING: Quality of writing ☆☆☆☆☆
Strength of characters ☆☆☆☆☆ Plot ☆☆☆☆☆

22. TITLE

Start date: _____ Finish date: _____

Author(s): _____

Publisher: _____ Year published: _____

Fiction/Genre: _____ or Nonfiction/Category: _____

Where I bought, borrowed, or found the book: _____

Main character(s) or subject: _____

My review and thoughts: _____

_____

_____

_____

_____

_____

_____

_____

_____

_____

_____

_____

OVERALL RATING: Quality of writing ☆☆☆☆☆
Strength of characters ☆☆☆☆☆ Plot ☆☆☆☆☆

23. TITLE

Start date: _____ Finish date: _____

Author(s): _____

Publisher: _____ Year published: _____

Fiction/Genre: _____ or Nonfiction/Category: _____

Where I bought, borrowed, or found the book: _____

Main character(s) or subject: _____

My review and thoughts: _____

_____

_____

_____

_____

_____

_____

_____

_____

_____

_____

_____

OVERALL RATING: Quality of writing ☆☆☆☆☆
Strength of characters ☆☆☆☆☆ Plot ☆☆☆☆☆

24. TITLE

Start date: _____ Finish date: _____

Author(s): _____

Publisher: _____ Year published: _____

Fiction/Genre: _____ or Nonfiction/Category: _____

Where I bought, borrowed, or found the book: _____

Main character(s) or subject: _____

My review and thoughts: _____

_____

_____

_____

_____

_____

_____

_____

_____

_____

_____

_____

OVERALL RATING: Quality of writing ☆☆☆☆☆
Strength of characters ☆☆☆☆☆ Plot ☆☆☆☆☆

25. TITLE

Start date: _____ Finish date: _____

Author(s): _____

Publisher: _____ Year published: _____

Fiction/Genre: _____ or Nonfiction/Category: _____

Where I bought, borrowed, or found the book: _____

Main character(s) or subject: _____

My review and thoughts: _____

_____

_____

_____

_____

_____

_____

_____

_____

_____

_____

_____

_____

OVERALL RATING: Quality of writing ☆☆☆☆☆
Strength of characters ☆☆☆☆☆ Plot ☆☆☆☆☆

26. TITLE

Start date: _____ Finish date: _____

Author(s): _____

Publisher: _____ Year published: _____

Fiction/Genre: _____ or Nonfiction/Category: _____

Where I bought, borrowed, or found the book: _____

Main character(s) or subject: _____

My review and thoughts: _____

_____

_____

_____

_____

_____

_____

_____

_____

_____

_____

_____

_____

OVERALL RATING: Quality of writing ☆☆☆☆☆
Strength of characters ☆☆☆☆☆ Plot ☆☆☆☆☆

27. TITLE

Start date: _____ Finish date: _____

Author(s): _____

Publisher: _____ Year published: _____

Fiction/Genre: _____ or Nonfiction/Category: _____

Where I bought, borrowed, or found the book: _____

Main character(s) or subject: _____

My review and thoughts: _____

_____

_____

_____

_____

_____

_____

_____

_____

_____

_____

_____

_____

OVERALL RATING: Quality of writing ☆☆☆☆☆
Strength of characters ☆☆☆☆☆ Plot ☆☆☆☆☆

28. TITLE

Start date: _____ Finish date: _____

Author(s): _____

Publisher: _____ Year published: _____

Fiction/Genre: _____ or Nonfiction/Category: _____

Where I bought, borrowed, or found the book: _____

Main character(s) or subject: _____

My review and thoughts: _____

_____

_____

_____

_____

_____

_____

_____

_____

_____

_____

_____

_____

OVERALL RATING: Quality of writing ☆☆☆☆☆
Strength of characters ☆☆☆☆☆ Plot ☆☆☆☆☆

29. TITLE

Start date: _____ Finish date: _____

Author(s): _____

Publisher: _____ Year published: _____

Fiction/Genre: _____ or Nonfiction/Category: _____

Where I bought, borrowed, or found the book: _____

Main character(s) or subject: _____

My review and thoughts: _____

_____

_____

_____

_____

_____

_____

_____

_____

_____

_____

_____

_____

OVERALL RATING: Quality of writing ☆☆☆☆☆
Strength of characters ☆☆☆☆☆ Plot ☆☆☆☆☆

30. TITLE

Start date: _____ Finish date: _____

Author(s): _____

Publisher: _____ Year published: _____

Fiction/Genre: _____ or Nonfiction/Category: _____

Where I bought, borrowed, or found the book: _____

Main character(s) or subject: _____

My review and thoughts: _____

_____

_____

_____

_____

_____

_____

_____

_____

_____

_____

_____

OVERALL RATING: Quality of writing ☆☆☆☆☆
Strength of characters ☆☆☆☆☆ Plot ☆☆☆☆☆

31. TITLE

Start date: _____ Finish date: _____

Author(s): _____

Publisher: _____ Year published: _____

Fiction/Genre: _____ or Nonfiction/Category: _____

Where I bought, borrowed, or found the book: _____

Main character(s) or subject: _____

My review and thoughts: _____

_____

_____

_____

_____

_____

_____

_____

_____

_____

_____

_____

OVERALL RATING: Quality of writing ☆☆☆☆☆
Strength of characters ☆☆☆☆☆ Plot ☆☆☆☆☆

32. TITLE

Start date: _____ Finish date: _____

Author(s): _____

Publisher: _____ Year published: _____

Fiction/Genre: _____ or Nonfiction/Category: _____

Where I bought, borrowed, or found the book: _____

Main character(s) or subject: _____

My review and thoughts: _____

_____

_____

_____

_____

_____

_____

_____

_____

_____

_____

_____

OVERALL RATING: Quality of writing ☆☆☆☆☆
Strength of characters ☆☆☆☆☆ Plot ☆☆☆☆☆

33. TITLE

Start date: _____ Finish date: _____

Author(s): _____

Publisher: _____ Year published: _____

Fiction/Genre: _____ or Nonfiction/Category: _____

Where I bought, borrowed, or found the book: _____

Main character(s) or subject: _____

My review and thoughts: _____

_____

_____

_____

_____

_____

_____

_____

_____

_____

_____

_____

_____

OVERALL RATING: Quality of writing ☆☆☆☆☆
Strength of characters ☆☆☆☆☆ Plot ☆☆☆☆☆

34. TITLE

Start date: _____ Finish date: _____

Author(s): _____

Publisher: _____ Year published: _____

Fiction/Genre: _____ or Nonfiction/Category: _____

Where I bought, borrowed, or found the book: _____

Main character(s) or subject: _____

My review and thoughts: _____

_____

_____

_____

_____

_____

_____

_____

_____

_____

_____

_____

OVERALL RATING: Quality of writing ☆☆☆☆☆
Strength of characters ☆☆☆☆☆ Plot ☆☆☆☆☆

35. TITLE

Start date: _____ Finish date: _____

Author(s): _____

Publisher: _____ Year published: _____

Fiction/Genre: _____ or Nonfiction/Category: _____

Where I bought, borrowed, or found the book: _____

Main character(s) or subject: _____

My review and thoughts: _____

_____

_____

_____

_____

_____

_____

_____

_____

_____

_____

_____

OVERALL RATING: Quality of writing ☆☆☆☆☆
Strength of characters ☆☆☆☆☆ Plot ☆☆☆☆☆

36. TITLE

Start date: _____ Finish date: _____

Author(s): _____

Publisher: _____ Year published: _____

Fiction/Genre: _____ or Nonfiction/Category: _____

Where I bought, borrowed, or found the book: _____

Main character(s) or subject: _____

My review and thoughts: _____

_____

_____

_____

_____

_____

_____

_____

_____

_____

_____

_____

OVERALL RATING: Quality of writing ☆☆☆☆☆
Strength of characters ☆☆☆☆☆ Plot ☆☆☆☆☆

37. TITLE

Start date: _____ Finish date: _____

Author(s): _____

Publisher: _____ Year published: _____

Fiction/Genre: _____ or Nonfiction/Category: _____

Where I bought, borrowed, or found the book: _____

Main character(s) or subject: _____

My review and thoughts: _____

_____

_____

_____

_____

_____

_____

_____

_____

_____

_____

_____

OVERALL RATING: Quality of writing ☆☆☆☆☆
Strength of characters ☆☆☆☆☆ Plot ☆☆☆☆☆

38. TITLE

Start date: _____ Finish date: _____

Author(s): _____

Publisher: _____ Year published: _____

Fiction/Genre: _____ or Nonfiction/Category: _____

Where I bought, borrowed, or found the book: _____

Main character(s) or subject: _____

My review and thoughts: _____

_____

_____

_____

_____

_____

_____

_____

_____

_____

_____

_____

OVERALL RATING: Quality of writing ☆☆☆☆☆
Strength of characters ☆☆☆☆☆ Plot ☆☆☆☆☆

39. TITLE

Start date: _____ Finish date: _____

Author(s): _____

Publisher: _____ Year published: _____

Fiction/Genre: _____ or Nonfiction/Category: _____

Where I bought, borrowed, or found the book: _____

Main character(s) or subject: _____

My review and thoughts: _____

_____

_____

_____

_____

_____

_____

_____

_____

_____

_____

_____

_____

OVERALL RATING: Quality of writing ☆☆☆☆☆
Strength of characters ☆☆☆☆☆ Plot ☆☆☆☆☆

40. TITLE

Start date: _____ Finish date: _____

Author(s): _____

Publisher: _____ Year published: _____

Fiction/Genre: _____ or Nonfiction/Category: _____

Where I bought, borrowed, or found the book: _____

Main character(s) or subject: _____

My review and thoughts: _____

_____

_____

_____

_____

_____

_____

_____

_____

_____

_____

_____

_____

OVERALL RATING: Quality of writing ☆☆☆☆☆
Strength of characters ☆☆☆☆☆ Plot ☆☆☆☆☆

41. TITLE

Start date: _____ Finish date: _____

Author(s): _____

Publisher: _____ Year published: _____

Fiction/Genre: _____ or Nonfiction/Category: _____

Where I bought, borrowed, or found the book: _____

Main character(s) or subject: _____

My review and thoughts: _____

_____

_____

_____

_____

_____

_____

_____

_____

_____

_____

_____

OVERALL RATING: Quality of writing ☆☆☆☆☆
Strength of characters ☆☆☆☆☆ Plot ☆☆☆☆☆

42. TITLE

Start date: _____ Finish date: _____

Author(s): _____

Publisher: _____ Year published: _____

Fiction/Genre: _____ or Nonfiction/Category: _____

Where I bought, borrowed, or found the book: _____

Main character(s) or subject: _____

My review and thoughts: _____

_____

_____

_____

_____

_____

_____

_____

_____

_____

_____

_____

_____

OVERALL RATING: Quality of writing ☆☆☆☆☆
Strength of characters ☆☆☆☆☆ Plot ☆☆☆☆☆

43. TITLE

Start date: _____ Finish date: _____

Author(s): _____

Publisher: _____ Year published: _____

Fiction/Genre: _____ or Nonfiction/Category: _____

Where I bought, borrowed, or found the book: _____

Main character(s) or subject: _____

My review and thoughts: _____

_____

_____

_____

_____

_____

_____

_____

_____

_____

_____

_____

OVERALL RATING: Quality of writing ☆☆☆☆☆
Strength of characters ☆☆☆☆☆ Plot ☆☆☆☆☆

44. TITLE

Start date: _____ Finish date: _____

Author(s): _____

Publisher: _____ Year published: _____

Fiction/Genre: _____ or Nonfiction/Category: _____

Where I bought, borrowed, or found the book: _____

Main character(s) or subject: _____

My review and thoughts: _____

_____

_____

_____

_____

_____

_____

_____

_____

_____

_____

_____

OVERALL RATING: Quality of writing ☆☆☆☆☆
Strength of characters ☆☆☆☆☆ Plot ☆☆☆☆☆

45. TITLE

Start date: _____ Finish date: _____

Author(s): _____

Publisher: _____ Year published: _____

Fiction/Genre: _____ or Nonfiction/Category: _____

Where I bought, borrowed, or found the book: _____

Main character(s) or subject: _____

My review and thoughts: _____

_____

_____

_____

_____

_____

_____

_____

_____

_____

_____

_____

_____

OVERALL RATING: Quality of writing ☆☆☆☆☆
Strength of characters ☆☆☆☆☆ Plot ☆☆☆☆☆

46. TITLE

Start date: _____ Finish date: _____

Author(s): _____

Publisher: _____ Year published: _____

Fiction/Genre: _____ or Nonfiction/Category: _____

Where I bought, borrowed, or found the book: _____

Main character(s) or subject: _____

My review and thoughts: _____

_____

_____

_____

_____

_____

_____

_____

_____

_____

_____

_____

OVERALL RATING: Quality of writing ☆☆☆☆☆
Strength of characters ☆☆☆☆☆ Plot ☆☆☆☆☆

47. TITLE

Start date: _____ Finish date: _____

Author(s): _____

Publisher: _____ Year published: _____

Fiction/Genre: _____ or Nonfiction/Category: _____

Where I bought, borrowed, or found the book: _____

Main character(s) or subject: _____

My review and thoughts: _____

_____

_____

_____

_____

_____

_____

_____

_____

_____

_____

_____

OVERALL RATING: Quality of writing ☆☆☆☆☆
Strength of characters ☆☆☆☆☆ Plot ☆☆☆☆☆

48. TITLE

Start date: _____ Finish date: _____

Author(s): _____

Publisher: _____ Year published: _____

Fiction/Genre: _____ or Nonfiction/Category: _____

Where I bought, borrowed, or found the book: _____

Main character(s) or subject: _____

My review and thoughts: _____

_____

_____

_____

_____

_____

_____

_____

_____

_____

_____

_____

_____

OVERALL RATING: Quality of writing ☆☆☆☆☆
Strength of characters ☆☆☆☆☆ Plot ☆☆☆☆☆

49. TITLE

Start date: _____ Finish date: _____

Author(s): _____

Publisher: _____ Year published: _____

Fiction/Genre: _____ or Nonfiction/Category: _____

Where I bought, borrowed, or found the book: _____

Main character(s) or subject: _____

My review and thoughts: _____

_____

_____

_____

_____

_____

_____

_____

_____

_____

_____

_____

OVERALL RATING: Quality of writing ☆☆☆☆☆
Strength of characters ☆☆☆☆☆ Plot ☆☆☆☆☆

50. TITLE

Start date: _____ Finish date: _____

Author(s): _____

Publisher: _____ Year published: _____

Fiction/Genre: _____ or Nonfiction/Category: _____

Where I bought, borrowed, or found the book: _____

Main character(s) or subject: _____

My review and thoughts: _____

_____

_____

_____

_____

_____

_____

_____

_____

_____

_____

_____

_____

OVERALL RATING: Quality of writing ☆☆☆☆☆
Strength of characters ☆☆☆☆☆ Plot ☆☆☆☆☆

51. TITLE

Start date: _____ Finish date: _____

Author(s): _____

Publisher: _____ Year published: _____

Fiction/Genre: _____ or Nonfiction/Category: _____

Where I bought, borrowed, or found the book: _____

Main character(s) or subject: _____

My review and thoughts: _____

_____

_____

_____

_____

_____

_____

_____

_____

_____

_____

_____

OVERALL RATING: Quality of writing ☆☆☆☆☆
Strength of characters ☆☆☆☆☆ Plot ☆☆☆☆☆

52. TITLE

Start date: _____ Finish date: _____

Author(s): _____

Publisher: _____ Year published: _____

Fiction/Genre: _____ or Nonfiction/Category: _____

Where I bought, borrowed, or found the book: _____

Main character(s) or subject: _____

My review and thoughts: _____

_____

_____

_____

_____

_____

_____

_____

_____

_____

_____

_____

OVERALL RATING: Quality of writing ☆☆☆☆☆
Strength of characters ☆☆☆☆☆ Plot ☆☆☆☆☆

53. TITLE

Start date: _____ Finish date: _____

Author(s): _____

Publisher: _____ Year published: _____

Fiction/Genre: _____ or Nonfiction/Category: _____

Where I bought, borrowed, or found the book: _____

Main character(s) or subject: _____

My review and thoughts: _____

_____

_____

_____

_____

_____

_____

_____

_____

_____

_____

_____

_____

OVERALL RATING: Quality of writing ☆☆☆☆☆
Strength of characters ☆☆☆☆☆ Plot ☆☆☆☆☆

54. TITLE

Start date: _____ Finish date: _____

Author(s): _____

Publisher: _____ Year published: _____

Fiction/Genre: _____ or Nonfiction/Category: _____

Where I bought, borrowed, or found the book: _____

Main character(s) or subject: _____

My review and thoughts: _____

_____

_____

_____

_____

_____

_____

_____

_____

_____

_____

_____

_____

OVERALL RATING: Quality of writing ☆☆☆☆☆
Strength of characters ☆☆☆☆☆ Plot ☆☆☆☆☆

55. TITLE

Start date: _____ Finish date: _____

Author(s): _____

Publisher: _____ Year published: _____

Fiction/Genre: _____ or Nonfiction/Category: _____

Where I bought, borrowed, or found the book: _____

Main character(s) or subject: _____

My review and thoughts: _____

_____

_____

_____

_____

_____

_____

_____

_____

_____

_____

_____

OVERALL RATING: Quality of writing ☆☆☆☆☆
Strength of characters ☆☆☆☆☆ Plot ☆☆☆☆☆

56. TITLE

Start date: _____ Finish date: _____

Author(s): _____

Publisher: _____ Year published: _____

Fiction/Genre: _____ or Nonfiction/Category: _____

Where I bought, borrowed, or found the book: _____

Main character(s) or subject: _____

My review and thoughts: _____

_____

_____

_____

_____

_____

_____

_____

_____

_____

_____

_____

OVERALL RATING: Quality of writing ☆☆☆☆☆
Strength of characters ☆☆☆☆☆ Plot ☆☆☆☆☆

57. TITLE

Start date: _____ Finish date: _____

Author(s): _____

Publisher: _____ Year published: _____

Fiction/Genre: _____ or Nonfiction/Category: _____

Where I bought, borrowed, or found the book: _____

Main character(s) or subject: _____

My review and thoughts: _____

_____

_____

_____

_____

_____

_____

_____

_____

_____

_____

_____

_____

OVERALL RATING: Quality of writing ☆☆☆☆☆
Strength of characters ☆☆☆☆☆ Plot ☆☆☆☆☆

58. TITLE

Start date: _____ Finish date: _____

Author(s): _____

Publisher: _____ Year published: _____

Fiction/Genre: _____ or Nonfiction/Category: _____

Where I bought, borrowed, or found the book: _____

Main character(s) or subject: _____

My review and thoughts: _____

_____

_____

_____

_____

_____

_____

_____

_____

_____

_____

_____

_____

OVERALL RATING: Quality of writing ☆☆☆☆☆
Strength of characters ☆☆☆☆☆ Plot ☆☆☆☆☆

59. TITLE

Start date: _____ Finish date: _____

Author(s): _____

Publisher: _____ Year published: _____

Fiction/Genre: _____ or Nonfiction/Category: _____

Where I bought, borrowed, or found the book: _____

Main character(s) or subject: _____

My review and thoughts: _____

_____

_____

_____

_____

_____

_____

_____

_____

_____

_____

_____

OVERALL RATING: Quality of writing ☆☆☆☆☆
Strength of characters ☆☆☆☆☆ Plot ☆☆☆☆☆

60. TITLE

Start date: _____ Finish date: _____

Author(s): _____

Publisher: _____ Year published: _____

Fiction/Genre: _____ or Nonfiction/Category: _____

Where I bought, borrowed, or found the book: _____

Main character(s) or subject: _____

My review and thoughts: _____

_____

_____

_____

_____

_____

_____

_____

_____

_____

_____

_____

OVERALL RATING: Quality of writing ☆☆☆☆☆
Strength of characters ☆☆☆☆☆ Plot ☆☆☆☆☆

61. TITLE

Start date: _____ Finish date: _____

Author(s): _____

Publisher: _____ Year published: _____

Fiction/Genre: _____ or Nonfiction/Category: _____

Where I bought, borrowed, or found the book: _____

Main character(s) or subject: _____

My review and thoughts: _____

_____

_____

_____

_____

_____

_____

_____

_____

_____

_____

_____

_____

OVERALL RATING: Quality of writing ☆☆☆☆☆
Strength of characters ☆☆☆☆☆ Plot ☆☆☆☆☆

62. TITLE

Start date: _____ Finish date: _____

Author(s): _____

Publisher: _____ Year published: _____

Fiction/Genre: _____ or Nonfiction/Category: _____

Where I bought, borrowed, or found the book: _____

Main character(s) or subject: _____

My review and thoughts: _____

_____

_____

_____

_____

_____

_____

_____

_____

_____

_____

_____

OVERALL RATING: Quality of writing ☆☆☆☆☆
Strength of characters ☆☆☆☆☆ Plot ☆☆☆☆☆

63. TITLE

Start date: _____ Finish date: _____

Author(s): _____

Publisher: _____ Year published: _____

Fiction/Genre: _____ or Nonfiction/Category: _____

Where I bought, borrowed, or found the book: _____

Main character(s) or subject: _____

My review and thoughts: _____

_____

_____

_____

_____

_____

_____

_____

_____

_____

_____

_____

_____

OVERALL RATING: Quality of writing ☆☆☆☆☆
Strength of characters ☆☆☆☆☆ Plot ☆☆☆☆☆

64. TITLE

Start date: _____ Finish date: _____

Author(s): _____

Publisher: _____ Year published: _____

Fiction/Genre: _____ or Nonfiction/Category: _____

Where I bought, borrowed, or found the book: _____

Main character(s) or subject: _____

My review and thoughts: _____

_____

_____

_____

_____

_____

_____

_____

_____

_____

_____

_____

_____

OVERALL RATING: Quality of writing ☆☆☆☆☆
Strength of characters ☆☆☆☆☆ Plot ☆☆☆☆☆

65. TITLE

Start date: _____ Finish date: _____

Author(s): _____

Publisher: _____ Year published: _____

Fiction/Genre: _____ or Nonfiction/Category: _____

Where I bought, borrowed, or found the book: _____

Main character(s) or subject: _____

My review and thoughts: _____

_____

_____

_____

_____

_____

_____

_____

_____

_____

_____

_____

OVERALL RATING: Quality of writing ☆☆☆☆☆
Strength of characters ☆☆☆☆☆ Plot ☆☆☆☆☆

66. TITLE

Start date: _____ Finish date: _____

Author(s): _____

Publisher: _____ Year published: _____

Fiction/Genre: _____ or Nonfiction/Category: _____

Where I bought, borrowed, or found the book: _____

Main character(s) or subject: _____

My review and thoughts: _____

_____

_____

_____

_____

_____

_____

_____

_____

_____

_____

_____

OVERALL RATING: Quality of writing ☆☆☆☆☆
Strength of characters ☆☆☆☆☆ Plot ☆☆☆☆☆

67. TITLE

Start date: _____ Finish date: _____

Author(s): _____

Publisher: _____ Year published: _____

Fiction/Genre: _____ or Nonfiction/Category: _____

Where I bought, borrowed, or found the book: _____

Main character(s) or subject: _____

My review and thoughts: _____

_____

_____

_____

_____

_____

_____

_____

_____

_____

_____

_____

_____

OVERALL RATING: Quality of writing ☆☆☆☆☆
Strength of characters ☆☆☆☆☆ Plot ☆☆☆☆☆

68. TITLE

Start date: _____ Finish date: _____

Author(s): _____

Publisher: _____ Year published: _____

Fiction/Genre: _____ or Nonfiction/Category: _____

Where I bought, borrowed, or found the book: _____

Main character(s) or subject: _____

My review and thoughts: _____

_____

_____

_____

_____

_____

_____

_____

_____

_____

_____

_____

_____

OVERALL RATING: Quality of writing ☆☆☆☆☆
Strength of characters ☆☆☆☆☆ Plot ☆☆☆☆☆

69. TITLE

Start date: _____ Finish date: _____

Author(s): _____

Publisher: _____ Year published: _____

Fiction/Genre: _____ or Nonfiction/Category: _____

Where I bought, borrowed, or found the book: _____

Main character(s) or subject: _____

My review and thoughts: _____

_____

_____

_____

_____

_____

_____

_____

_____

_____

_____

_____

OVERALL RATING: Quality of writing ☆☆☆☆☆
Strength of characters ☆☆☆☆☆ Plot ☆☆☆☆☆

70. TITLE

Start date: _____ Finish date: _____

Author(s): _____

Publisher: _____ Year published: _____

Fiction/Genre: _____ or Nonfiction/Category: _____

Where I bought, borrowed, or found the book: _____

Main character(s) or subject: _____

My review and thoughts: _____

_____

_____

_____

_____

_____

_____

_____

_____

_____

_____

_____

_____

OVERALL RATING: Quality of writing ☆☆☆☆☆
Strength of characters ☆☆☆☆☆ Plot ☆☆☆☆☆

71. TITLE

Start date: _____ Finish date: _____

Author(s): _____

Publisher: _____ Year published: _____

Fiction/Genre: _____ or Nonfiction/Category: _____

Where I bought, borrowed, or found the book: _____

Main character(s) or subject: _____

My review and thoughts: _____

_____

_____

_____

_____

_____

_____

_____

_____

_____

_____

_____

_____

OVERALL RATING: Quality of writing ☆☆☆☆☆
Strength of characters ☆☆☆☆☆ Plot ☆☆☆☆☆

72. TITLE

Start date: _____ Finish date: _____

Author(s): _____

Publisher: _____ Year published: _____

Fiction/Genre: _____ or Nonfiction/Category: _____

Where I bought, borrowed, or found the book: _____

Main character(s) or subject: _____

My review and thoughts: _____

_____

_____

_____

_____

_____

_____

_____

_____

_____

_____

_____

OVERALL RATING: Quality of writing ☆☆☆☆☆
Strength of characters ☆☆☆☆☆ Plot ☆☆☆☆☆

73. TITLE

Start date: _____ Finish date: _____

Author(s): _____

Publisher: _____ Year published: _____

Fiction/Genre: _____ or Nonfiction/Category: _____

Where I bought, borrowed, or found the book: _____

Main character(s) or subject: _____

My review and thoughts: _____

_____

_____

_____

_____

_____

_____

_____

_____

_____

_____

_____

OVERALL RATING: Quality of writing ☆☆☆☆☆
Strength of characters ☆☆☆☆☆ Plot ☆☆☆☆☆

74. TITLE

Start date: _____ Finish date: _____

Author(s): _____

Publisher: _____ Year published: _____

Fiction/Genre: _____ or Nonfiction/Category: _____

Where I bought, borrowed, or found the book: _____

Main character(s) or subject: _____

My review and thoughts: _____

_____

_____

_____

_____

_____

_____

_____

_____

_____

_____

_____

_____

_____

OVERALL RATING: Quality of writing ☆☆☆☆☆
Strength of characters ☆☆☆☆☆ Plot ☆☆☆☆☆

75. TITLE

Start date: _____ Finish date: _____

Author(s): _____

Publisher: _____ Year published: _____

Fiction/Genre: _____ or Nonfiction/Category: _____

Where I bought, borrowed, or found the book: _____

Main character(s) or subject: _____

My review and thoughts: _____

_____

_____

_____

_____

_____

_____

_____

_____

_____

_____

_____

_____

OVERALL RATING: Quality of writing ☆☆☆☆☆
Strength of characters ☆☆☆☆☆ Plot ☆☆☆☆☆

76. TITLE

Start date: _____ Finish date: _____

Author(s): _____

Publisher: _____ Year published: _____

Fiction/Genre: _____ or Nonfiction/Category: _____

Where I bought, borrowed, or found the book: _____

Main character(s) or subject: _____

My review and thoughts: _____

_____

_____

_____

_____

_____

_____

_____

_____

_____

_____

_____

OVERALL RATING: Quality of writing ☆☆☆☆☆
Strength of characters ☆☆☆☆☆ Plot ☆☆☆☆☆

77. TITLE

Start date: _____ Finish date: _____

Author(s): _____

Publisher: _____ Year published: _____

Fiction/Genre: _____ or Nonfiction/Category: _____

Where I bought, borrowed, or found the book: _____

Main character(s) or subject: _____

My review and thoughts: _____

_____

_____

_____

_____

_____

_____

_____

_____

_____

_____

_____

OVERALL RATING: Quality of writing ☆☆☆☆☆
Strength of characters ☆☆☆☆☆ Plot ☆☆☆☆☆

78. TITLE

Start date: _____ Finish date: _____

Author(s): _____

Publisher: _____ Year published: _____

Fiction/Genre: _____ or Nonfiction/Category: _____

Where I bought, borrowed, or found the book: _____

Main character(s) or subject: _____

My review and thoughts: _____

_____

_____

_____

_____

_____

_____

_____

_____

_____

_____

_____

_____

OVERALL RATING: Quality of writing ☆☆☆☆☆
Strength of characters ☆☆☆☆☆ Plot ☆☆☆☆☆

79. TITLE

Start date: _____ Finish date: _____

Author(s): _____

Publisher: _____ Year published: _____

Fiction/Genre: _____ or Nonfiction/Category: _____

Where I bought, borrowed, or found the book: _____

Main character(s) or subject: _____

My review and thoughts: _____

_____

_____

_____

_____

_____

_____

_____

_____

_____

_____

_____

_____

OVERALL RATING: Quality of writing ☆☆☆☆☆
Strength of characters ☆☆☆☆☆ Plot ☆☆☆☆☆

80. TITLE

Start date: _____ Finish date: _____

Author(s): _____

Publisher: _____ Year published: _____

Fiction/Genre: _____ or Nonfiction/Category: _____

Where I bought, borrowed, or found the book: _____

Main character(s) or subject: _____

My review and thoughts: _____

_____

_____

_____

_____

_____

_____

_____

_____

_____

_____

_____

_____

OVERALL RATING: Quality of writing ☆☆☆☆☆
Strength of characters ☆☆☆☆☆ Plot ☆☆☆☆☆

81. TITLE

Start date: _____ Finish date: _____

Author(s): _____

Publisher: _____ Year published: _____

Fiction/Genre: _____ or Nonfiction/Category: _____

Where I bought, borrowed, or found the book: _____

Main character(s) or subject: _____

My review and thoughts: _____

_____

_____

_____

_____

_____

_____

_____

_____

_____

_____

_____

OVERALL RATING: Quality of writing ☆☆☆☆☆
Strength of characters ☆☆☆☆☆ Plot ☆☆☆☆☆

82. TITLE

Start date: _____ Finish date: _____

Author(s): _____

Publisher: _____ Year published: _____

Fiction/Genre: _____ or Nonfiction/Category: _____

Where I bought, borrowed, or found the book: _____

Main character(s) or subject: _____

My review and thoughts: _____

_____

_____

_____

_____

_____

_____

_____

_____

_____

_____

_____

_____

OVERALL RATING: Quality of writing ☆☆☆☆☆
Strength of characters ☆☆☆☆☆ Plot ☆☆☆☆☆

83. TITLE

Start date: _____ Finish date: _____

Author(s): _____

Publisher: _____ Year published: _____

Fiction/Genre: _____ or Nonfiction/Category: _____

Where I bought, borrowed, or found the book: _____

Main character(s) or subject: _____

My review and thoughts: _____

_____

_____

_____

_____

_____

_____

_____

_____

_____

_____

_____

OVERALL RATING: Quality of writing ☆☆☆☆☆
Strength of characters ☆☆☆☆☆ Plot ☆☆☆☆☆

84. TITLE

Start date: _____ Finish date: _____

Author(s): _____

Publisher: _____ Year published: _____

Fiction/Genre: _____ or Nonfiction/Category: _____

Where I bought, borrowed, or found the book: _____

Main character(s) or subject: _____

My review and thoughts: _____

_____

_____

_____

_____

_____

_____

_____

_____

_____

_____

_____

OVERALL RATING: Quality of writing ☆☆☆☆☆
Strength of characters ☆☆☆☆☆ Plot ☆☆☆☆☆

85. TITLE

Start date: _____ Finish date: _____

Author(s): _____

Publisher: _____ Year published: _____

Fiction/Genre: _____ or Nonfiction/Category: _____

Where I bought, borrowed, or found the book: _____

Main character(s) or subject: _____

My review and thoughts: _____

_____

_____

_____

_____

_____

_____

_____

_____

_____

_____

_____

OVERALL RATING: Quality of writing ☆☆☆☆☆
Strength of characters ☆☆☆☆☆ Plot ☆☆☆☆☆

86. TITLE

Start date: _____ Finish date: _____

Author(s): _____

Publisher: _____ Year published: _____

Fiction/Genre: _____ or Nonfiction/Category: _____

Where I bought, borrowed, or found the book: _____

Main character(s) or subject: _____

My review and thoughts: _____

_____

_____

_____

_____

_____

_____

_____

_____

_____

_____

_____

OVERALL RATING: Quality of writing ☆☆☆☆☆
Strength of characters ☆☆☆☆☆ Plot ☆☆☆☆☆

87. TITLE

Start date: _____ Finish date: _____

Author(s): _____

Publisher: _____ Year published: _____

Fiction/Genre: _____ or Nonfiction/Category: _____

Where I bought, borrowed, or found the book: _____

Main character(s) or subject: _____

My review and thoughts: _____

_____

_____

_____

_____

_____

_____

_____

_____

_____

_____

_____

_____

OVERALL RATING: Quality of writing ☆☆☆☆☆
Strength of characters ☆☆☆☆☆ Plot ☆☆☆☆☆

88. TITLE

Start date: _____ Finish date: _____

Author(s): _____

Publisher: _____ Year published: _____

Fiction/Genre: _____ or Nonfiction/Category: _____

Where I bought, borrowed, or found the book: _____

Main character(s) or subject: _____

My review and thoughts: _____

_____

_____

_____

_____

_____

_____

_____

_____

_____

_____

_____

_____

OVERALL RATING: Quality of writing ☆☆☆☆☆
Strength of characters ☆☆☆☆☆ Plot ☆☆☆☆☆

89. TITLE

Start date: _____ Finish date: _____

Author(s): _____

Publisher: _____ Year published: _____

Fiction/Genre: _____ or Nonfiction/Category: _____

Where I bought, borrowed, or found the book: _____

Main character(s) or subject: _____

My review and thoughts: _____

_____

_____

_____

_____

_____

_____

_____

_____

_____

_____

_____

OVERALL RATING: Quality of writing ☆☆☆☆☆
Strength of characters ☆☆☆☆☆ Plot ☆☆☆☆☆

90. TITLE

Start date: _____ Finish date: _____

Author(s): _____

Publisher: _____ Year published: _____

Fiction/Genre: _____ or Nonfiction/Category: _____

Where I bought, borrowed, or found the book: _____

Main character(s) or subject: _____

My review and thoughts: _____

_____

_____

_____

_____

_____

_____

_____

_____

_____

_____

_____

OVERALL RATING: Quality of writing ☆☆☆☆☆
Strength of characters ☆☆☆☆☆ Plot ☆☆☆☆☆

91. TITLE

Start date: _____ Finish date: _____

Author(s): _____

Publisher: _____ Year published: _____

Fiction/Genre: _____ or Nonfiction/Category: _____

Where I bought, borrowed, or found the book: _____

Main character(s) or subject: _____

My review and thoughts: _____

_____

_____

_____

_____

_____

_____

_____

_____

_____

_____

_____

_____

OVERALL RATING: Quality of writing ☆☆☆☆☆
Strength of characters ☆☆☆☆☆ Plot ☆☆☆☆☆

92. TITLE

Start date: _____ Finish date: _____

Author(s): _____

Publisher: _____ Year published: _____

Fiction/Genre: _____ or Nonfiction/Category: _____

Where I bought, borrowed, or found the book: _____

Main character(s) or subject: _____

My review and thoughts: _____

_____

_____

_____

_____

_____

_____

_____

_____

_____

_____

_____

_____

OVERALL RATING: Quality of writing ☆☆☆☆☆
Strength of characters ☆☆☆☆☆ Plot ☆☆☆☆☆

93. TITLE

Start date: _____ Finish date: _____

Author(s): _____

Publisher: _____ Year published: _____

Fiction/Genre: _____ or Nonfiction/Category: _____

Where I bought, borrowed, or found the book: _____

Main character(s) or subject: _____

My review and thoughts: _____

_____

_____

_____

_____

_____

_____

_____

_____

_____

_____

_____

OVERALL RATING: Quality of writing ☆☆☆☆☆
Strength of characters ☆☆☆☆☆ Plot ☆☆☆☆☆

94. TITLE

Start date: _____ Finish date: _____

Author(s): _____

Publisher: _____ Year published: _____

Fiction/Genre: _____ or Nonfiction/Category: _____

Where I bought, borrowed, or found the book: _____

Main character(s) or subject: _____

My review and thoughts: _____

_____

_____

_____

_____

_____

_____

_____

_____

_____

_____

_____

OVERALL RATING: Quality of writing ☆☆☆☆☆
Strength of characters ☆☆☆☆☆ Plot ☆☆☆☆☆

95. TITLE

Start date: _____ Finish date: _____

Author(s): _____

Publisher: _____ Year published: _____

Fiction/Genre: _____ or Nonfiction/Category: _____

Where I bought, borrowed, or found the book: _____

Main character(s) or subject: _____

My review and thoughts: _____

_____

_____

_____

_____

_____

_____

_____

_____

_____

_____

_____

_____

OVERALL RATING: Quality of writing ☆☆☆☆☆
Strength of characters ☆☆☆☆☆ Plot ☆☆☆☆☆

96. TITLE

Start date: _____ Finish date: _____

Author(s): _____

Publisher: _____ Year published: _____

Fiction/Genre: _____ or Nonfiction/Category: _____

Where I bought, borrowed, or found the book: _____

Main character(s) or subject: _____

My review and thoughts: _____

_____

_____

_____

_____

_____

_____

_____

_____

_____

_____

_____

OVERALL RATING: Quality of writing ☆☆☆☆☆
Strength of characters ☆☆☆☆☆ Plot ☆☆☆☆☆

97. TITLE

Start date: _____ Finish date: _____

Author(s): _____

Publisher: _____ Year published: _____

Fiction/Genre: _____ or Nonfiction/Category: _____

Where I bought, borrowed, or found the book: _____

Main character(s) or subject: _____

My review and thoughts: _____

_____

_____

_____

_____

_____

_____

_____

_____

_____

_____

_____

OVERALL RATING: Quality of writing ☆☆☆☆☆
Strength of characters ☆☆☆☆☆ Plot ☆☆☆☆☆

98. TITLE

Start date: _____ Finish date: _____

Author(s): _____

Publisher: _____ Year published: _____

Fiction/Genre: _____ or Nonfiction/Category: _____

Where I bought, borrowed, or found the book: _____

Main character(s) or subject: _____

My review and thoughts: _____

_____

_____

_____

_____

_____

_____

_____

_____

_____

_____

OVERALL RATING: Quality of writing ☆☆☆☆☆
Strength of characters ☆☆☆☆☆ Plot ☆☆☆☆☆

99. TITLE

Start date: _____ Finish date: _____

Author(s): _____

Publisher: _____ Year published: _____

Fiction/Genre: _____ or Nonfiction/Category: _____

Where I bought, borrowed, or found the book: _____

Main character(s) or subject: _____

My review and thoughts: _____

_____

_____

_____

_____

_____

_____

_____

_____

_____

_____

_____

OVERALL RATING: Quality of writing ☆☆☆☆☆
Strength of characters ☆☆☆☆☆ Plot ☆☆☆☆☆

100. TITLE

Start date: _____ Finish date: _____

Author(s): _____

Publisher: _____ Year published: _____

Fiction/Genre: _____ or Nonfiction/Category: _____

Where I bought, borrowed, or found the book: _____

Main character(s) or subject: _____

My review and thoughts: _____

_____

_____

_____

_____

_____

_____

_____

_____

_____

_____

_____

OVERALL RATING: Quality of writing ☆☆☆☆☆
Strength of characters ☆☆☆☆☆ Plot ☆☆☆☆☆

24 BOOK
CHALLENGES

"There is no Frigate like a Book
To take us Lands away."

—Emily Dickinson

24 BOOK CHALLENGES

☐ 1. A book written by someone on a different continent

Title: _____

Author(s): _____

Publisher: _____ Year published: _____

Notes: _____

_____

_____

_____

_____

_____

_____

_____

_____

_____

_____

_____

_____

_____

_____

24 BOOK CHALLENGES

☐ **2. A book written before 1900**

Title: _____

Author(s): _____

Publisher: _____ Year published: _____

Notes: _____

_____

_____

_____

_____

_____

_____

_____

_____

_____

_____

_____

_____

_____

_____

24 BOOK CHALLENGES

❑ 3. A book of poetry

Title: _____

Author(s): _____

Publisher: _____ Year published: _____

Notes: _____

_____

_____

_____

_____

_____

_____

_____

_____

_____

_____

_____

_____

_____

24 BOOK CHALLENGES

❏ **4. A graphic novel**

Title: _____

Author(s): _____

Publisher: _____ Year published: _____

Notes: _____

_____

_____

_____

_____

_____

_____

_____

_____

_____

_____

_____

_____

_____

_____

_____

24 BOOK CHALLENGES

☐ 5. A book set in wartime

Title: _____

Author(s): _____

Publisher: _____ Year published: _____

Notes: _____

_____

_____

_____

_____

_____

_____

_____

_____

_____

_____

_____

_____

_____

_____

24 BOOK CHALLENGES

❏ **6. A book recently turned into a movie or TV show**

Title: _____

Author(s): _____

Publisher: _____ Year published: _____

Notes: _____

_____

_____

_____

_____

_____

_____

_____

_____

_____

_____

_____

_____

_____

_____

24 BOOK CHALLENGES

❑ 7. A book set in a dystopian future

Title: _____

Author(s): _____

Publisher: _____ Year published: _____

Notes: _____

_____

_____

_____

_____

_____

_____

_____

_____

_____

_____

_____

_____

_____

_____

_____

_____

24 BOOK CHALLENGES

❑ **8. A book set in a time period you would like to visit**

Title: _____

Author(s): _____

Publisher: _____ Year published: _____

Notes: _____

_____

_____

_____

_____

_____

_____

_____

_____

_____

_____

_____

_____

_____

24 BOOK CHALLENGES

Title: _____

Author(s): _____

Publisher: _____ Year published: _____

Notes: _____

_____

_____

_____

_____

_____

_____

_____

_____

_____

_____

_____

_____

_____

_____

24 BOOK CHALLENGES

☐ **10. A book by or about someone you admire**

Title: _____

Author(s): _____

Publisher: _____ Year published:_____

Notes: _____

_____

_____

_____

_____

_____

_____

_____

_____

_____

_____

_____

_____

_____

_____

_____

24 BOOK CHALLENGES

❏ 11. A book about religion or spirituality

Title: _____

Author(s): _____

Publisher: _____ Year published: _____

Notes: _____

_____

_____

_____

_____

_____

_____

_____

_____

_____

_____

_____

_____

_____

24 BOOK CHALLENGES

❏ 12. A book of short stories

Title: _____

Author(s): _____

Publisher: _____ Year published: _____

Notes: _____

_____

_____

_____

_____

_____

_____

_____

_____

_____

_____

_____

_____

_____

_____

_____

_____

24 BOOK CHALLENGES

❏ **13. A book set in a country you would like to visit**

Title: _____

Author(s): _____

Publisher: _____ Year published:_____

Notes: _____

_____

_____

_____

_____

_____

_____

_____

_____

_____

_____

_____

_____

_____

_____

24 BOOK CHALLENGES

❏ 14. A guilty-pleasure beach book

Title: _____

Author(s): _____

Publisher: _____ Year published:_____

Notes: _____

_____

_____

_____

_____

_____

_____

_____

_____

_____

_____

_____

_____

_____

_____

24 BOOK CHALLENGES

❏ 15. A book written the year you were born

Title: _____

Author(s): _____

Publisher: _____ Year published: _____

Notes: _____

_____

_____

_____

_____

_____

_____

_____

_____

_____

_____

_____

_____

_____

24 BOOK CHALLENGES

❏ **16. A mystery**

Title: _____

Author(s): _____

Publisher: _____ Year published: _____

Notes: _____

_____

_____

_____

_____

_____

_____

_____

_____

_____

_____

_____

_____

_____

_____

_____

24 BOOK CHALLENGES

❑ **17. A book about or narrated by a child**

Title: _____

Author(s): _____

Publisher: _____ Year published: _____

Notes: _____

_____

_____

_____

_____

_____

_____

_____

_____

_____

_____

_____

_____

_____

_____

_____

24 BOOK CHALLENGES

☐ 18. A ghost story or scary book

Title: _____

Author(s): _____

Publisher: _____ Year published: _____

Notes: _____

_____

_____

_____

_____

_____

_____

_____

_____

_____

_____

_____

_____

_____

_____

_____

_____

_____

24 BOOK CHALLENGES

❏ **19. A memoir or biography**

Title: _____

Author(s): _____

Publisher: _____ Year published: _____

Notes: _____

_____

_____

_____

_____

_____

_____

_____

_____

_____

_____

_____

_____

_____

_____

24 BOOK CHALLENGES

❏ 20. A book on politics

Title: _____

Author(s): _____

Publisher: _____ Year published: _____

Notes: _____

_____

_____

_____

_____

_____

_____

_____

_____

_____

_____

_____

_____

_____

_____

24 BOOK CHALLENGES

❑ **21. A book about spies**

Title: _____

Author(s): _____

Publisher: _____ Year published:_____

Notes: _____

_____

_____

_____

_____

_____

_____

_____

_____

_____

_____

_____

_____

_____

_____

_____

24 BOOK CHALLENGES

❏ **22. A romance**

Title: _____

Author(s): _____

Publisher: _____ Year published: _____

Notes: _____

_____

_____

_____

_____

_____

_____

_____

_____

_____

_____

_____

_____

_____

_____

24 BOOK CHALLENGES

❏ **23. A fantasy**

Title: _____

Author(s): _____

Publisher: _____ Year published: _____

Notes: _____

_____

_____

_____

_____

_____

_____

_____

_____

_____

_____

_____

_____

_____

_____

_____

24 BOOK CHALLENGES

☐ **24. A thriller**

Title: _____

Author(s): _____

Publisher: _____ Year published: _____

Notes: _____

_____

_____

_____

_____

_____

_____

_____

_____

_____

_____

_____

_____

_____

_____

MY BOOK LISTS

"The reading of all good books
is like conversation with the
finest [people] of the past centuries."

—Descartes

MY BOOK LISTS

10 Favorite Books of All Time

1. Title: _____

   Author: _____ Reason: _____

2. Title: _____

   Author: _____ Reason: _____

3. Title: _____

   Author: _____ Reason: _____

4. Title: _____

   Author: _____ Reason: _____

5. Title: _____

   Author: _____ Reason: _____

6. Title: _____

   Author: _____ Reason: _____

7. Title: _____

   Author: _____ Reason: _____

8. Title: _____

   Author: _____ Reason: _____

9. Title: _____

   Author: _____ Reason: _____

10. Title: _____

    Author: _____ Reason: _____

MY BOOK LISTS

10 Favorite Characters

1. Title: _____

    Name of Character: _____

2. Title: _____

    Name of Character: _____

3. Title: _____

    Name of Character: _____

4. Title: _____

    Name of Character: _____

5. Title: _____

    Name of Character: _____

6. Title: _____

    Name of Character: _____

7. Title: _____

    Name of Character: _____

8. Title: _____

    Name of Character: _____

9. Title: _____

    Name of Character: _____

10. Title: _____

    Name of Character: _____

MY BOOK LISTS

10 Favorite Villains

1. Title: _____

   Name of Character: _____

2. Title: _____

   Name of Character: _____

3. Title: _____

   Name of Character: _____

4. Title: _____

   Name of Character: _____

5. Title: _____

   Name of Character: _____

6. Title: _____

   Name of Character: _____

7. Title: _____

   Name of Character: _____

8. Title: _____

   Name of Character: _____

9. Title: _____

   Name of Character: _____

10. Title: _____

    Name of Character: _____

MY BOOK LISTS

10 Favorite Book First Sentences

1. Title: _____
   Sentence: _____
2. Title: _____
   Sentence: _____
3. Title: _____
   Sentence: _____
4. Title: _____
   Sentence: _____
5. Title: _____
   Sentence: _____
6. Title: _____
   Sentence: _____
7. Title: _____
   Sentence: _____
8. Title: _____
   Sentence: _____
9. Title: _____
   Sentence: _____
10. Title: _____
    Sentence: _____

MY BOOK LISTS

10 Favorite Book Last Sentences

1. Title: _____
    Sentence: _____

2. Title: _____
    Sentence: _____

3. Title: _____
    Sentence: _____

4. Title: _____
    Sentence: _____

5. Title: _____
    Sentence: _____

6. Title: _____
    Sentence: _____

7. Title: _____
    Sentence: _____

8. Title: _____
    Sentence: _____

9. Title: _____
    Sentence: _____

10. Title: _____
    Sentence: _____

MY BOOK LISTS

10 Favorite Childhood Books

1. Title: _Charlie + the Chocolate Factory_
   Author: _Rhoald Dahl_ Memory: _Summer Book_
2. Title: _____
   Author: _____ Memory: _____
3. Title: _____
   Author: _____ Memory: _____
4. Title: _____
   Author: _____ Memory: _____
5. Title: _____
   Author: _____ Memory: _____
6. Title: _____
   Author: _____ Memory: _____
7. Title: _____
   Author: _____ Memory: _____
8. Title: _____
   Author: _____ Memory: _____
9. Title: _____
   Author: _____ Memory: _____
10. Title: _____
    Author: _____ Memory: _____

MY BOOK LISTS

10 Books I Would Bring to a Desert Island

1. Title: _____
   Author: _____ Reason: _____

2. Title: _____
   Author: _____ Reason: _____

3. Title: _____
   Author: _____ Reason: _____

4. Title: _____
   Author: _____ Reason: _____

5. Title: _____
   Author: _____ Reason: _____

6. Title: _____
   Author: _____ Reason: _____

7. Title: _____
   Author: _____ Reason: _____

8. Title: _____
   Author: _____ Reason: _____

9. Title: _____
   Author: _____ Reason: _____

10. Title: _____
    Author: _____ Reason: _____

MY BOOK LISTS

10 Favorite Books I Have Re-read

1. Title: _____

   Author: _____ Reason: _____

2. Title: _____

   Author: _____ Reason: _____

3. Title: _____

   Author: _____ Reason: _____

4. Title: _____

   Author: _____ Reason: _____

5. Title: _____

   Author: _____ Reason: _____

6. Title: _____

   Author: _____ Reason: _____

7. Title: _____

   Author: _____ Reason: _____

8. Title: _____

   Author: _____ Reason: _____

9. Title: _____

   Author: _____ Reason: _____

10. Title: _____

   Author: _____ Reason: _____

MY BOOK LISTS

10 Favorite Classics

1. Title: _____
   Author: _____ Reason: _____

2. Title: _____
   Author: _____ Reason: _____

3. Title: _____
   Author: _____ Reason: _____

4. Title: _____
   Author: _____ Reason: _____

5. Title: _____
   Author: _____ Reason: _____

6. Title: _____
   Author: _____ Reason: _____

7. Title: _____
   Author: _____ Reason: _____

8. Title: _____
   Author: _____ Reason: _____

9. Title: _____
   Author: _____ Reason: _____

10. Title: _____
    Author: _____ Reason: _____

MY BOOK LISTS

10 Favorite Books by Contemporary Authors

1. Title: _____
   Author: _____ Reason: _____
2. Title: _____
   Author: _____ Reason: _____
3. Title: _____
   Author: _____ Reason: _____
4. Title: _____
   Author: _____ Reason: _____
5. Title: _____
   Author: _____ Reason: _____
6. Title: _____
   Author: _____ Reason: _____
7. Title: _____
   Author: _____ Reason: _____
8. Title: _____
   Author: _____ Reason: _____
9. Title: _____
   Author: _____ Reason: _____
10. Title: _____
    Author: _____ Reason: _____

MY BOOK LISTS

10 Favorite Memoirs or Biographies

1. Title: _____
   Author: _____ Reason: _____

2. Title: _____
   Author: _____ Reason: _____

3. Title: _____
   Author: _____ Reason: _____

4. Title: _____
   Author: _____ Reason: _____

5. Title: _____
   Author: _____ Reason: _____

6. Title: _____
   Author: _____ Reason: _____

7. Title: _____
   Author: _____ Reason: _____

8. Title: _____
   Author: _____ Reason: _____

9. Title: _____
   Author: _____ Reason: _____

10. Title: _____
    Author: _____ Reason: _____

MY BOOK LISTS

10 Longest Books I Have Read

1. Title: _____

    Author: _____ Reason: _____

2. Title: _____

    Author: _____ Reason: _____

3. Title: _____

    Author: _____ Reason: _____

4. Title: _____

    Author: _____ Reason: _____

5. Title: _____

    Author: _____ Reason: _____

6. Title: _____

    Author: _____ Reason: _____

7. Title: _____

    Author: _____ Reason: _____

8. Title: _____

    Author: _____ Reason: _____

9. Title: _____

    Author: _____ Reason: _____

10. Title: _____

    Author: _____ Reason: _____

MY BOOK LISTS

10 Worst Books I Have Read

1. Title: _____
   Author: _____ Reason: _____

2. Title: _____
   Author: _____ Reason: _____

3. Title: _____
   Author: _____ Reason: _____

4. Title: _____
   Author: _____ Reason: _____

5. Title: _____
   Author: _____ Reason: _____

6. Title: _____
   Author: _____ Reason: _____

7. Title: _____
   Author: _____ Reason: _____

8. Title: _____
   Author: _____ Reason: _____

9. Title: _____
   Author: _____ Reason: _____

10. Title: _____
    Author: _____ Reason: _____

MY BOOK LISTS

10 Favorite Poems

1. Title: _____
   Author: _____ Reason: _____
2. Title: _____
   Author: _____ Reason: _____
3. Title: _____
   Author: _____ Reason: _____
4. Title: _____
   Author: _____ Reason: _____
5. Title: _____
   Author: _____ Reason: _____
6. Title: _____
   Author: _____ Reason: _____
7. Title: _____
   Author: _____ Reason: _____
8. Title: _____
   Author: _____ Reason: _____
9. Title: _____
   Author: _____ Reason: _____
10. Title: _____
    Author: _____ Reason: _____

MY BOOK LISTS

10 Favorite Movies or TV Shows Based on Books

1. Name of Book: _____

   Name of Movie or Show: _____

2. Name of Book: _____

   Name of Movie or Show: _____

3. Name of Book: _____

   Name of Movie or Show: _____

4. Name of Book: _____

   Name of Movie or Show: _____

5. Name of Book: _____

   Name of Movie or Show: _____

6. Name of Book: _____

   Name of Movie or Show: _____

7. Name of Book: _____

   Name of Movie or Show: _____

8. Name of Book: _____

   Name of Movie or Show: _____

9. Name of Book: _____

   Name of Movie or Show: _____

10. Name of Book: _____

    Name of Movie or Show: _____

MY BOOK LISTS

10 Funniest Books I Have Read

1. Title: _____
   Author: _____ Reason: _____
2. Title: _____
   Author: _____ Reason: _____
3. Title: _____
   Author: _____ Reason: _____
4. Title: _____
   Author: _____ Reason: _____
5. Title: _____
   Author: _____ Reason: _____
6. Title: _____
   Author: _____ Reason: _____
7. Title: _____
   Author: _____ Reason: _____
8. Title: _____
   Author: _____ Reason: _____
9. Title: _____
   Author: _____ Reason: _____
10. Title: _____
    Author: _____ Reason: _____

MY BOOK LISTS

10 Saddest Books I Have Read

1. Title: _____
   Author: _____ Reason: _____

2. Title: _____
   Author: _____ Reason: _____

3. Title: _____
   Author: _____ Reason: _____

4. Title: _____
   Author: _____ Reason: _____

5. Title: _____
   Author: _____ Reason: _____

6. Title: _____
   Author: _____ Reason: _____

7. Title: _____
   Author: _____ Reason: _____

8. Title: _____
   Author: _____ Reason: _____

9. Title: _____
   Author: _____ Reason: _____

10. Title: _____
    Author: _____ Reason: _____

MY BOOK LISTS

10 Scariest Books I Have Read

1. Title: _____
   Author: _____ Reason: _____

2. Title: _____
   Author: _____ Reason: _____

3. Title: _____
   Author: _____ Reason: _____

4. Title: _____
   Author: _____ Reason: _____

5. Title: _____
   Author: _____ Reason: _____

6. Title: _____
   Author: _____ Reason: _____

7. Title: _____
   Author: _____ Reason: _____

8. Title: _____
   Author: _____ Reason: _____

9. Title: _____
   Author: _____ Reason: _____

10. Title: _____
    Author: _____ Reason: _____

MY BOOK LISTS

10 Most Suspenseful Books I Have Read

1. Title: _____
   Author: _____ Reason: _____

2. Title: _____
   Author: _____ Reason: _____

3. Title: _____
   Author: _____ Reason: _____

4. Title: _____
   Author: _____ Reason: _____

5. Title: _____
   Author: _____ Reason: _____

6. Title: _____
   Author: _____ Reason: _____

7. Title: _____
   Author: _____ Reason: _____

8. Title: _____
   Author: _____ Reason: _____

9. Title: _____
   Author: _____ Reason: _____

10. Title: _____
    Author: _____ Reason: _____

MY BOOK LISTS

10 Most Romantic Books I Have Read

1. Title: _____

    Author: _____ Reason: _____

2. Title: _____

    Author: _____ Reason: _____

3. Title: _____

    Author: _____ Reason: _____

4. Title: _____

    Author: _____ Reason: _____

5. Title: _____

    Author: _____ Reason: _____

6. Title: _____

    Author: _____ Reason: _____

7. Title: _____

    Author: _____ Reason: _____

8. Title: _____

    Author: _____ Reason: _____

9. Title: _____

    Author: _____ Reason: _____

10. Title: _____

    Author: _____ Reason: _____

MY BOOK LISTS

10 Books That Taught Me the Most or Changed My Thinking

1. Title: _____

   Author: _____ Reason: _____

2. Title: _____

   Author: _____ Reason: _____

3. Title: _____

   Author: _____ Reason: _____

4. Title: _____

   Author: _____ Reason: _____

5. Title: _____

   Author: _____ Reason: _____

6. Title: _____

   Author: _____ Reason: _____

7. Title: _____

   Author: _____ Reason: _____

8. Title: _____

   Author: _____ Reason: _____

9. Title: _____

   Author: _____ Reason: _____

10. Title: _____

    Author: _____ Reason: _____

MY BOOK LISTS

10 Authors I Would Invite to Dinner

1. Title: _____

   Author: _____ Reason: _____

2. Title: _____

   Author: _____ Reason: _____

3. Title: _____

   Author: _____ Reason: _____

4. Title: _____

   Author: _____ Reason: _____

5. Title: _____

   Author: _____ Reason: _____

6. Title: _____

   Author: _____ Reason: _____

7. Title: _____

   Author: _____ Reason: _____

8. Title: _____

   Author: _____ Reason: _____

9. Title: _____

   Author: _____ Reason: _____

10. Title: _____

    Author: _____ Reason: _____

MY BOOK LISTS

10 Books with the Coolest Titles

1. Title: _____

   Author: _____ Reason: _____

2. Title: _____

   Author: _____ Reason: _____

3. Title: _____

   Author: _____ Reason: _____

4. Title: _____

   Author: _____ Reason: _____

5. Title: _____

   Author: _____ Reason: _____

6. Title: _____

   Author: _____ Reason: _____

7. Title: _____

   Author: _____ Reason: _____

8. Title: _____

   Author: _____ Reason: _____

9. Title: _____

   Author: _____ Reason: _____

10. Title: _____

    Author: _____ Reason: _____

MY BOOK LISTS

10 Books with the Coolest Covers

1. Title: _____

   Author: _____ Reason: _____

2. Title: _____

   Author: _____ Reason: _____

3. Title: _____

   Author: _____ Reason: _____

4. Title: _____

   Author: _____ Reason: _____

5. Title: _____

   Author: _____ Reason: _____

6. Title: _____

   Author: _____ Reason: _____

7. Title: _____

   Author: _____ Reason: _____

8. Title: _____

   Author: _____ Reason: _____

9. Title: _____

   Author: _____ Reason: _____

10. Title: _____

    Author: _____ Reason: _____

BEST BOOK LISTS
PRIZEWINNERS AND CLASSICS

"To read well, that is, to read true books
in a true spirit, is a noble exercise."

—Henry David Thoreau

The Modern Library—100 Best Novels

- [ ] 1. *Ulysses*, James Joyce
- [ ] 2. *The Great Gatsby*, F. Scott Fitzgerald
- [ ] 3. *A Portrait of the Artist As a Young Man*, James Joyce
- [ ] 4. *Lolita*, Vladimir Nabokov
- [ ] 5. *Brave New World*, Aldous Huxley
- [ ] 6. *The Sound and the Fury*, William Faulkner
- [ ] 7. *Catch-22*, Joseph Heller
- [ ] 8. *Darkness at Noon*, Arthur Koestler
- [ ] 9. *Sons and Lovers*, D. H. Lawrence
- [ ] 10. *The Grapes of Wrath*, John Steinbeck
- [ ] 11. *Under the Volcano*, Malcolm Lowry
- [ ] 12. *The Way of All Flesh*, Samuel Butler
- [ ] 13. *1984*, George Orwell
- [ ] 14. *I, Claudius*, Robert Graves
- [ ] 15. *To the Lighthouse*, Virginia Woolf
- [ ] 16. *An American Tragedy*, Theodore Dreiser
- [ ] 17. *The Heart Is a Lonely Hunter*, Carson McCullers
- [ ] 18. *Slaughterhouse-Five*, Kurt Vonnegut
- [ ] 19. *Invisible Man*, Ralph Ellison
- [ ] 20. *Native Son*, Richard Wright
- [ ] 21. *Henderson the Rain King*, Saul Bellow
- [ ] 22. *Appointment in Samarra*, John O'Hara
- [ ] 23. *U.S.A. (trilogy)*, John Dos Passos
- [ ] 24. *Winesburg, Ohio*, Sherwood Anderson
- [ ] 25. *A Passage to India*, E. M. Forster
- [ ] 26. *The Wings of the Dove*, Henry James
- [ ] 27. *The Ambassadors*, Henry James
- [ ] 28. *Tender Is the Night*, F. Scott Fitzgerald
- [ ] 29. *Studs Lonigan (trilogy)*, James T. Farrell
- [ ] 30. *The Good Soldier*, Ford Madox Ford
- [ ] 31. *Animal Farm*, George Orwell
- [ ] 32. *The Golden Bowl*, Henry James

The Modern Library—100 Best Books of Nonfiction

Pulitzer Prize for Fiction

[Years skipped indicate no awards given that year]

☐ **1918** *His Family*, Ernest Poole
☐ **1919** *The Magnificent Ambersons*, Booth Tarkington
☐ **1921** *The Age of Innocence*, Edith Wharton
☐ **1922** *Alice Adams*, Booth Tarkington
☐ **1923** *One of Ours*, Willa Cather
☐ **1924** *The Able McLaughlins*, Margaret Wilson
☐ **1925** *So Big*, Edna Ferber
☐ **1926** *Arrowsmith*, Sinclair Lewis (declined prize)
☐ **1927** *Early Autumn*, Louis Bromfield
☐ **1928** *The Bridge of San Luis Rey*, Thornton Wilder
☐ **1929** *Scarlet Sister Mary*, Julia Peterkin
☐ **1930** *Laughing Boy*, Oliver La Farge
☐ **1931** *Years of Grace*, Margaret Ayer Barnes
☐ **1932** *The Good Earth*, Pearl S. Buck
☐ **1933** *The Store*, Thomas Sigismund Stribling
☐ **1934** *Lamb in His Bosom*, Caroline Miller
☐ **1935** *Now in November*, Josephine Winslow Johnson
☐ **1936** *Honey in the Horn*, Harold L. Davis
☐ **1937** *Gone with the Wind*, Margaret Mitchell
☐ **1938** *The Late George Apley*, John Phillips Marquand
☐ **1939** *The Yearling*, Marjorie Kinnan Rawlings
☐ **1940** *The Grapes of Wrath*, John Steinbeck
☐ **1942** *In This Our Life*, Ellen Glasgow
☐ **1943** *Dragon's Teeth*, Upton Sinclair
☐ **1944** *Journey in the Dark*, Martin Flavin
☐ **1945** *A Bell for Adano*, John Hersey
☐ **1947** *All the King's Men*, Robert Penn Warren
☐ **1948** *Tales of the South Pacific*, James A. Michener
☐ **1949** *Guard of Honor*, James Gould Cozzens
☐ **1950** *The Way West*, A. B. Guthrie Jr.

- ☐ **1951** *The Town*, Conrad Richter
- ☐ **1952** *The Caine Mutiny*, Herman Wouk
- ☐ **1953** *The Old Man and the Sea*, Ernest Hemingway
- ☐ **1955** *A Fable*, William Faulkner
- ☐ **1956** *Andersonville*, MacKinlay Kantor
- ☐ **1958** *A Death in the Family*, James Agee (posthumous win)
- ☐ **1959** *The Travels of Jaimie McPheeters*, Robert Lewis Taylor
- ☐ **1960** *Advise and Consent*, Allen Drury
- ☐ **1961** *To Kill a Mockingbird*, Harper Lee
- ☐ **1962** *The Edge of Sadness*, Edwin O'Connor
- ☐ **1963** *The Reivers*, William Faulkner (posthumous win)
- ☐ **1965** *The Keepers of the House*, Shirley Ann Grau
- ☐ **1966** *The Collected Stories of Katherine Anne Porter*, Katherine Anne Porter
- ☐ **1967** *The Fixer*, Bernard Malamud
- ☐ **1968** *The Confessions of Nat Turner*, William Styron
- ☐ **1969** *House Made of Dawn*, N. Scott Momaday
- ☐ **1970** *The Collected Stories of Jean Stafford*, Jean Stafford
- ☐ **1972** *Angle of Repose*, Wallace Stegner
- ☐ **1973** *The Optimist's Daughter*, Eudora Welty
- ☐ **1975** *The Killer Angels*, Michael Shaara
- ☐ **1976** *Humboldt's Gift*, Saul Bellow
- ☐ **1977** No award given (*Roots*, Alex Haley, special Pulitzer Prize)
- ☐ **1978** *Elbow Room*, James Alan McPherson
- ☐ **1979** *The Stories of John Cheever*, John Cheever
- ☐ **1980** *The Executioner's Song*, Norman Mailer
- ☐ **1981** *A Confederacy of Dunces*, John Kennedy Toole (posthumous win)
- ☐ **1982** *Rabbit Is Rich*, John Updike
- ☐ **1983** *The Color Purple*, Alice Walker
- ☐ **1984** *Ironweed*, William Kennedy
- ☐ **1985** *Foreign Affairs*, Alison Lurie
- ☐ **1986** *Lonesome Dove*, Larry McMurtry
- ☐ **1987** *A Summons to Memphis*, Peter Taylor
- ☐ **1988** *Beloved*, Toni Morrison
- ☐ **1989** *Breathing Lessons*, Anne Tyler

- ☐ **1990** *The Mambo Kings Play Songs of Love*, Oscar Hijuelos
- ☐ **1991** *Rabbit at Rest*, John Updike
- ☐ **1992** *A Thousand Acres*, Jane Smiley
- ☐ **1993** *A Good Scent from a Strange Mountain*, Robert Olen Butler
- ☐ **1994** *The Shipping News*, E. Annie Proulx
- ☐ **1995** *The Stone Diaries*, Carol Shields
- ☐ **1996** *Independence Day*, Richard Ford
- ☐ **1997** *Martin Dressler: The Tale of an American Dreamer*, Steven Millhauser
- ☐ **1998** *American Pastoral*, Philip Roth
- ☐ **1999** *The Hours*, Michael Cunningham
- ☐ **2000** *Interpreter of Maladies*, Jhumpa Lahiri
- ☐ **2001** *The Amazing Adventures of Kavalier & Clay*, Michael Chabon
- ☐ **2002** *Empire Falls*, Richard Russo
- ☐ **2003** *Middlesex*, Jeffrey Eugenides
- ☐ **2004** *The Known World*, Edward P. Jones
- ☐ **2005** *Gilead*, Marilynne Robinson
- ☐ **2006** *March*, Geraldine Brooks
- ☐ **2007** *The Road*, Cormac McCarthy
- ☐ **2008** *The Brief Wondrous Life of Oscar Wao*, Junot Díaz
- ☐ **2009** *Olive Kitteridge*, Elizabeth Strout
- ☐ **2010** *Tinkers*, Paul Harding
- ☐ **2011** *A Visit From the Goon Squad*, Jennifer Egan
- ☐ **2013** *The Orphan Master's Son*, Adam Johnson
- ☐ **2014** *The Goldfinch*, Donna Tartt
- ☐ **2015** *All the Light We Cannot See*, Anthony Doerr
- ☐ **2016** *The Sympathizer*, Viet Thanh Nguyen
- ☐ **2017** *The Underground Railroad*, Colson Whitehead
- ☐ **2018** *Less*, Andrew Sean Greer

Man Booker Prize for Fiction

☐ **1997** *The God of Small Things*, Arundhati Roy
☐ **1969** *Something to Answer For*, P. H. Newby
☐ **1970** *The Elected Member*, Bernice Rubens
☐ **1970** (retrospective award) *Troubles*, J. G. Farrell
☐ **1971** *In a Free State*, V. S. Naipaul
☐ **1972** *G.*, John Berger
☐ **1973** *The Siege of Krishnapur*, J. G. Farrell
☐ **1974** *The Conservationist*, Nadine Gordimer, and
☐   *Holiday*, Stanley Middleton
☐ **1975** *Heat and Dust*, Ruth Prawer Jhabvala
☐ **1976** *Saville*, David Storey
☐ **1977** *Staying On*, Paul Scott
☐ **1978** *The Sea, the Sea*, Iris Murdoch
☐ **1979** *Offshore*, Penelope Fitzgerald
☐ **1980** *Rites of Passage*, William Golding
☐ **1981** *Midnight's Children*, Salman Rushdie
☐ **1982** *Schindler's Ark (Schindler's List)*, Thomas Keneally
☐ **1983** *Life & Times of Michael K*, J. M. Coetzee
☐ **1984** *Hotel du Lac*, Anita Brookner
☐ **1985** *The Bone People*, Keri Hulme
☐ **1986** *The Old Devils*, Kingsley Amis
☐ **1987** *Moon Tiger*, Penelope Lively
☐ **1988** *Oscar and Lucinda*, Peter Carey
☐ **1989** *The Remains of the Day*, Kazuo Ishiguro
☐ **1990** *Possession*, A. S. Byatt
☐ **1991** *The Famished Road*, Ben Okri
☐ **1992** *The English Patient*, Michael Ondaatje, and
☐   *Sacred Hunger*, Barry Unsworth
☐ **1993** *Paddy Clarke Ha Ha Ha*, Roddy Doyle
☐ **1994** *How Late It Was, How Late*, James Kelman
☐ **1995** *The Ghost Road*, Pat Barker

- ☐ **1996** *Last Orders*, Graham Swift
- ☐ **1998** *Amsterdam*, Ian McEwan
- ☐ **1999** *Disgrace*, J. M. Coetzee
- ☐ **2000** *The Blind Assassin*, Margaret Atwood
- ☐ **2001** *True History of the Kelly Gang*, Peter Carey
- ☐ **2002** *Life of Pi*, Yann Martel
- ☐ **2003** *Vernon God Little*, DBC Pierre
- ☐ **2004** *The Line of Beauty*, Alan Hollinghurst
- ☐ **2005** *The Sea*, John Banville
- ☐ **2006** *The Inheritance of Loss*, Kiran Desai
- ☐ **2007** *The Gathering*, Anne Enright
- ☐ **2008** *The White Tiger*, Aravind Adiga
- ☐ **2009** *Wolf Hall*, Hilary Mantel
- ☐ **2010** *The Finkler Question*, Howard Jacobson
- ☐ **2011** *The Sense of an Ending*, Julian Barnes
- ☐ **2012** *Bring Up the Bodies*, Hilary Mantel
- ☐ **2013** *The Luminaries*, Eleanor Catton
- ☐ **2014** *The Narrow Road to the Deep North*, Richard Flanagan
- ☐ **2015** *A Brief History of Seven Killings*, Marlon James
- ☐ **2016** *The Sellout*, Paul Beatty
- ☐ **2017** *Lincoln in the Bardo*, George Saunders
- ☐ **2018** *Milkman*, Anna Burns

BOOK CLUB
READING LIST

1. Title: _____

   Author: _____ Discussion Date: _____

2. Title: _____

   Author: _____ Discussion Date: _____

3. Title: _____

   Author: _____ Discussion Date: _____

4. Title: _____

   Author: _____ Discussion Date: _____

5. Title: _____

   Author: _____ Discussion Date: _____

6. Title: _____

   Author: _____ Discussion Date: _____

7. Title: _____

   Author: _____ Discussion Date: _____

8. Title: _____

   Author: _____ Discussion Date: _____

9. Title: _____

   Author: _____ Discussion Date: _____

10. Title: _____

   Author: _____ Discussion Date: _____

BOOK CLUB READING LIST

11. Title: _____

    Author: _____ Discussion Date: _____

12. Title: _____

    Author: _____ Discussion Date: _____

13. Title: _____

    Author: _____ Discussion Date: _____

14. Title: _____

    Author: _____ Discussion Date: _____

15. Title: _____

    Author: _____ Discussion Date: _____

16. Title: _____

    Author: _____ Discussion Date: _____

17. Title: _____

    Author: _____ Discussion Date: _____

18. Title: _____

    Author: _____ Discussion Date: _____

19. Title: _____

    Author: _____ Discussion Date: _____

20. Title: _____

    Author: _____ Discussion Date: _____

BOOK CLUB QUESTIONS

1. What did you like best about this book?

2. What did you like least about this book?

3. How did you find the quality of writing?

4. Which were your favorite characters?

5. Which were your least favorite characters?

6. Which character did you relate to the most?

7. If you were making a movie or television series based on this book, who would you cast in the starring roles?

8. What other books by this author have you read? Did you like them more or less than this book?

9. Would you read another book by this author? Why or why not?

10. What themes did the author emphasize throughout the book?

11. What did you think of the plot development?

12. What did you think of the book's ending?

13. How authentic were the characters and their dialogue?

14. How authentic is the culture, setting, or time period represented in the book?

15. What is your major take-away about the author's message?

BOOK CLUB NOTES

BOOK CLUB NOTES

WISH LIST OF BOOKS TO READ

"I read my eyes out
and can't read half enough . . .
The more one reads the more one sees
we have to read."

—John Adams

WISH LIST OF BOOKS TO READ

WISH LIST OF BOOKS TO READ

WISH LIST OF BOOKS TO READ

WISH LIST OF BOOKS TO READ

WISH LIST OF BOOKS TO READ

WISH LIST OF BOOKS TO READ

WISH LIST OF BOOKS TO READ

WISH LIST OF BOOKS TO READ